Contents

A beautiful Gentoo Penguin standing against an Antarctic landscape.

PENGUINS

Penguins are birds. Like all other birds, they have wings and are covered in feathers. They are also *warm-blooded* animals that lay eggs. It is said that they evolved from flying birds over 40 million years ago.

ANATOMY

Penguins are also *seabirds or marine* birds. This means that they spend most of their time in the ocean. Their bodies are made for swimming.

Penguins' feathers keep them warm and dry. They are, however, *flightless* bird. Unlike most other birds, they cannot fly. They have wings, but these are shaped like *flippers*. Their powerful flipper-like wings enable them to swim swiftly through the water.

Although penguins are great swimmers, they cannot stay underwater for long. They are, however, able to stay for up to 20 minutes under water without coming up for air. This enables them to be amazing deep sea divers.

Penguins fluffing their feathers to cool down.

HABITAT

Today, there are 17 *species* or types of penguins in the world. All of these penguins live in the Southern Hemisphere. Not all of them, however, live in the Antarctic.

Different species live in different *climates*. Some species, such as *Galapagos Penguins*, live on warm, *tropical* islands close to the equator. *Emperor Penguins* live only in the chilly Antarctic. Penguins are also found around the shores of Africa, South America, Australia, and New Zealand.

Penguins enjoying a chilly Antarctic habitat.

A penguin's perfect eyesight makes it a superior hunter.

SENSES

Penguins are said to be nearsighted on land. This means that they can only see objects that are close to them. Underwater, however, penguins have crystal clear vision.

Penguins use vocalizations, called calls or songs to communicate with each other. They vocalize to defend their territories and warn their colony about predators. They also use calls to find their mates and babies.

Even though they have no visible ears, penguins have incredible hearing. A mother penguin can pick out the call of her baby from among 10,000 other birds.

Chinstrap Penguins eating snow on a glacier.

FEEDING

Penguins are carnivores. They eat only the flesh of other animals. Penguins eat seafood, which they hunt. They can feed deep underwater. Their diet includes fish, a small shrimp-like creature called krill, and crustaceans.

Penguins have hooked beaks and rough tongues like velcro brushes. These stop their slippery food or prey from escaping.

Penguins do not drink water, but eat snow instead. A gland in their noses helps take out salt from the snow they eat and from the ocean water they may swallow when they catch fish.

MOVEMENT

Penguins' *torpedo-shaped* bodies and their flipper-like wings help them to fly through the water as fast as 15 mph (miles per hour).

In the water they are as graceful as birds in flight. On land, however, they look awkward as they seem to waddle along. What looks like waddling is actually a penguin taking very short steps to go from place to place.

They also hop and use their tails to help them in steep climbs. The *Rockhopper* Penguin, for example, jumps from rock to rock.

A penguin gliding gracefully through the blue ocean.

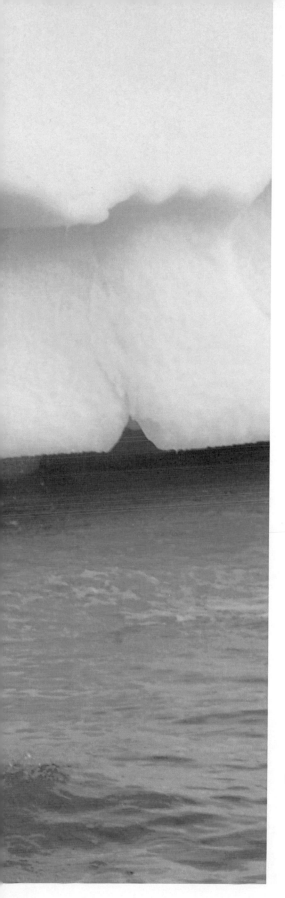

PLAY

Penguins love to have fun. They have been seen standing in rows taking turns to dive deep into the water. Swimming in the depths of the ocean is one of their favourite pastimes.

Like dolphins and whales, penguins have also been seen *flying* out of the water. This is called *porpoising or breaching*. It is said that penguins porpoise for the sheer delight of being in the water.

Penguins are also great surfers. They often ride a wave onto land. Penguins found in Antarctica have also been known to *toboggan* on their bellies and flippers through ice and snow.

Geronimo! Penguins having loads of fun.

COLONIES

Penguins are the most social of all birds. Penguins usually swim and live together in groups or colonies. These colonies can have tens of thousands of birds. The largest colonies may have millions of members.

Penguins living in cold regions keep each other warm by travelling in colonies. As they travel huddled together, they constantly move and swap places. This is so that every penguin gets a turn to keep warm as it moves into the center of the group.

A massive colony of King Penguins.

A group of Gentoo Penguins: a few nesting and one vocalizing.

MATING

Places where penguins mate, nest, and raise their chicks are called *rookeries*. These nesting places are found close to the shore and may be thousands of years old.

Each penguin species has different *mating rituals*. Male penguins show that they are ready to mate by calling out loud and strutting about to attract a female. They may arch their backs and stretch their wings. These behaviors are called *displays*.

Emperor Penguins have the most interesting displays. They start out with the male making a sound to get a female's attention. When the couple finds each other, they begin to walk among thousands of other penguins copying each other's movements. As a grand finale, they face each other and bow.

An endangered Jackass Penguin guarding its eggs.

EGGS

Like all birds, penguin chicks hatch from eggs. Each penguin species has eggs that differ in color, size, and shape. Penguins usually lay only one or two eggs at a time.

Penguins pip when they are ready to hatch. Pips are small cracks or holes that are made by chicks using their beaks. After the first pip, penguin chicks take about three days to chip their way out of the egg.

CARING FOR YOUNG

Penguins depend on both their parents to stay alive. From the time they are born they sing to their parents so that the parents learn to recognise their voice.

Adult penguins feed only their own chick or chicks. They feed their chicks with *regurgitated* food. To regurgitate is to cough up partially digested food from the belly. The parents pour this liquid meal into their chick's open mouth.

Parent penguins also *brood* chicks. This means that they keep them warm by covering them with a *brood pouch*. Penguins' brood pouches are warm layers of feathered skin, which help to keep eggs or chicks cosy.

A mother penguin feeding her young.

ADELIE PENGUINS

Adelie Penguins and Emperor Penguins are found only in Antarctica and its surrounding waters. Adelie Penguins are the smallest of the species found in this part of the world. They are also known as the Tuxedo Penguins of Antarctica.

These penguins build nests of stones on the rocky beaches of Antarctica. They look like happy chaps, but they are often found fighting over stones and the best rocks on which to build their stony nests.

Happy feet: Adelie Penguin dancing on a snowy shore.

African penguins queuing up.

AFRICAN PENGUINS

African Penguins or Blackfoot Penguins live on the coast of South Africa. They nest in burrows. These burrows provide protection from predators and the sun's hot rays.

These penguins are also called *Jackass Penguins* because their noisy calls sound like braying donkeys.

Notice this vocalizing penguin's chinstrap.

CHINSTRAP PENGUINS

Chinstrap Penguins get their names from the black band that runs under their chins. They are also known as *Ringed Penguins* and *Bearded Penguins*. These penguins are one of the most common penguin species. They are found on large icebergs and in the open ocean of the Antarctic region.

Despite their small size, they are very brave. The most aggressive of all penguin species, they often fight penguins much larger than themselves.

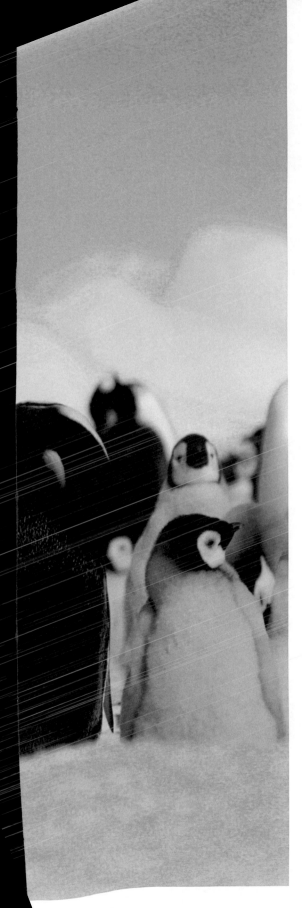

EMPEROR PENGUINS

Emperor Penguins are the largest penguins in the world. They are found only in Antarctica. They stand 3 feet (90 centimeters) tall and weigh over 100 pounds (45 kilograms).

While most birds have their young or *breed* in spring, Emperor Penguins breed in winter. During this time females lay a single egg. They then leave the eggs in the care of their mates and travel for many miles in search of food.

The males balance the eggs in their brood pouch for 65 days. They eat nothing and stand very still in the bitter cold.

After the eggs hatch, the mothers return with food to feed their chicks. If the mothers have not returned by the time the chicks hatch, the fathers will produce a regurgitated liquid known as *penguin milk* to feed the chicks.

A family of Emperor Penguins huddling together.

A Galapagos Penguin getting ready to take a dip.

GALAPAGOS PENGUINS

Galapagos Penguins are warm weather penguins. They live on the hot desert island of Galapagos. These penguins live close to the equator. They are able to survive because of cold-water currents that come to the island from Antarctica.

A King Penguin conference.

KING PENGUINS

King Penguins are the second largest penguins and are the most colourful penguins in the world. They have black heads and white bellies. They also have grey feathers on their backs and orange patches on their necks and the sides of their heads.

King Penguins do not waddle, hop, or slide on their bellies on land. Instead, they run on their feet. They are found in large colonies all year round because it takes 15 to 18 months to raise a single chick.

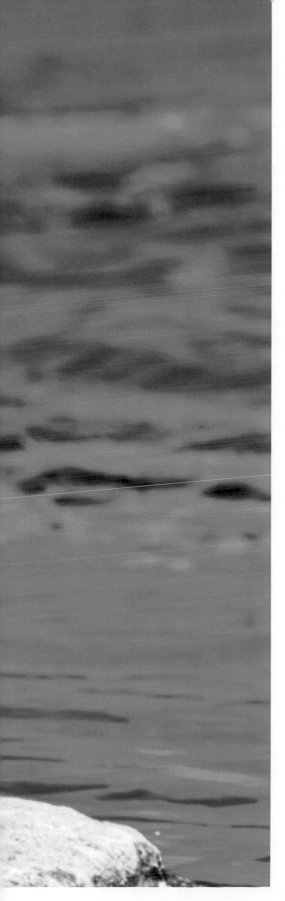

LITTLE BLUE PENGUINS

Little Blue Penguins are also called *Fairy Penguins*. They are the smallest penguins in the world. They are 1 foot (30 centimeters) tall and weigh about four pounds (1.5 kilograms).

These penguins get their names from the bluish-grey feathers on their backs. They have dark grey beaks and pinkish feet. They are found only in Australia and New Zealand and are known as the oldest of all the penguins.

Little Blue Penguins build their nests in rocky burrows. They have the widest range of songs compared to all other penguin species.

A Little Blue Penguin surveying the blue water.

A pair of Magallenic Penguins emerging from their burrows.

MAGELLANIC PENGUINS

Magellanic Penguins are named after the famous explorer Ferdinand Magellan. He discovered these penguins on his first voyage around the tip of South America.

These penguins live on the coast of Chile, Argentina, and the Falkland Islands. They are of average size and the largest *warm weather* penguins.

In the mating season Magellanic Penguins dig burrows under the ground. They form huge underground nesting colonies or *cities*, just like gophers.

A portrait of the "bad tempered" Rockhopper Penguin.

ROCKHOPPER PENGUINS

Rockhopper Penguins are found in the sub-Antarctic and regions of the Indian and South Atlantic oceans. Rockhopper Penguins have decorative yellow feather tufts on their heads. They have red eyes and sharp beaks.

Rockhopper penguins build nests on steep rocky slopes. They get their name from their strange ability to jump from rock to rock to their nesting places. They keep both feet together as they hop along.

These birds are 2 feet (60 centimeters) tall, but can hop up to 5 feet (1.5 meters). These penguins are tough and aggressive. They will attack anything that disturbs them.

A lone Humboldt Penguin standing on a rock.

PROTECT THE PENGUINS

Penguins are in trouble because of human activity. Overfishing has reduced their food supply. Pollution, oil spills, the introduction of predators, and humans taking over their breeding grounds have caused penguins to rapidly disappear.

Increasing awareness of these matters will help protect these much-loved creatures.

OUR AMAZING WORLD

COLLECT THEM ALL

WWW.OURAMAZINGWORLDBOOKS.COM

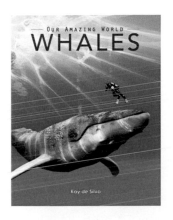

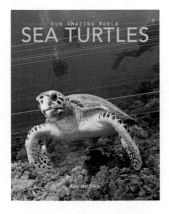

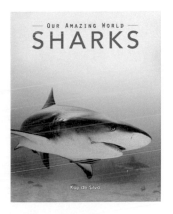

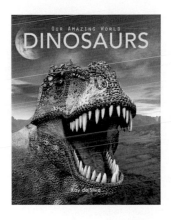

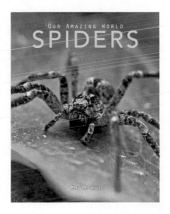

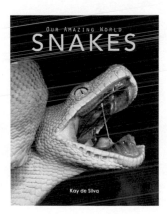

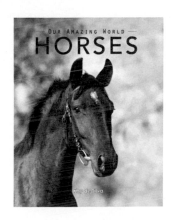

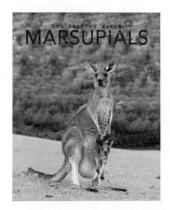

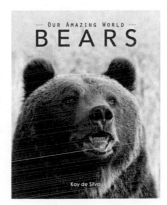

Aurora
An imprint of CKTY Publishing Solutions

www.ouramazingworldbooks.com

Made in the USA
San Bernardino, CA
31 January 2017